MULTIPLY BY HAND

The Nine Facts

Marcia S. Freeman

www.rourkeclassroom.com

D1361321

www.rourkepublishing.com

PHOTO CREDITS: All Photos © Renee Brady

Editor: Robert Stengard-Olliges

Cover design by Nicola Stratford, bdpublishing.com

Library of Congress Cataloging-in-Publication Data

Freeman, Marcia S. (Marcia Sheehan), 1937-
  Multiply by hand : the nines facts / Marcia S. Freeman.
     p. cm. -- (Math focal points)
  Includes index.
  ISBN 978-1-60044-643-6 (Hardcover)
  ISBN 978-1-60044-687-0 (Softcover)
  ISBN 978-1-60472-055-6 (Lap Book)
  ISBN 978-1-60472-106-5 (eBook)
  1. Multiplication--Juvenile literature. 2. Nine (The number)--Juvenile literature. I. Title.

  QA115.F74 2008
  513.2'13--dc22
                                    2007018019

Rourke Publishing
Printed in the United States of America, North Mankato, Minnesota
030411
030411LP-B

www.rourkepublishing.com - rourke@rourkepublishing.com
Post Office Box 643328 Vero Beach, Florida 32964

Table of Contents

Using Your Fingers in Math

Did you use your fingers to count when you were in kindergarten? Our fingers can be **handy** when it comes to math.

You may have used your fingers when you first learned to add.

Multiplying-by-Nine Finger Trick

1x9=9	6x9=54
2x9=18	7x9=63
3x9=27	8x9=72
4x9=36	9x9=81
5x9=45	10x9=90

Did you know you can use your fingers to learn how to multiply by nine? Here's how.

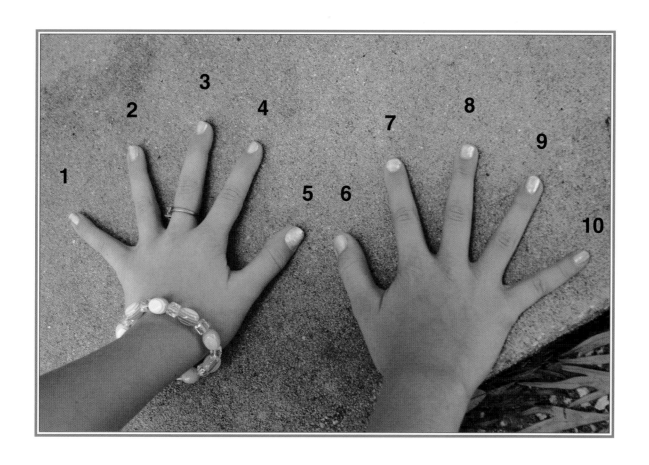

Spread your hands just like the hands in
the picture.

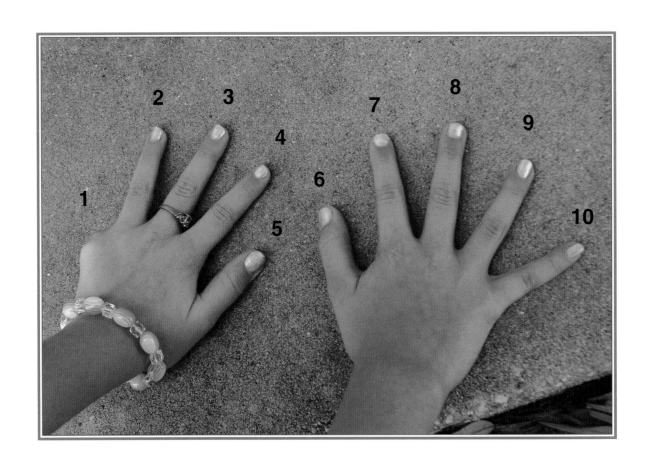

Curl down finger #1, your left hand **pinky**.
Count the fingers that are sticking up.

1x9=9	6x9=54
2x9=18	7x9=63
3x9=27	8x9=72
4x9=36	9x9=81
5x9=45	10x9=90

Did you count nine? That's right. One times nine equals nine. You can write that as: 1 X 9 = 9.

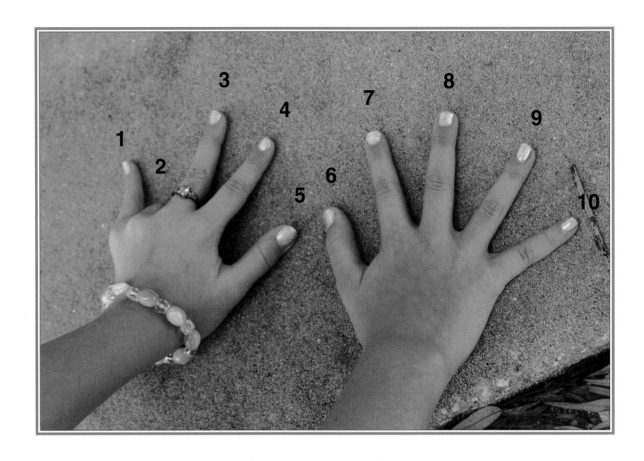

Now curl down finger #2. You will have one finger sticking up on the left side of the curled down finger. Count eight fingers sticking up on the right.

1x9=9	6x9=54
2x9=18	7x9=63
3x9=27	8x9=72
4x9=36	9x9=81
5x9=45	10x9=90

The fingers on the left **represent** the ten's place and the fingers on the right represent the one's place.

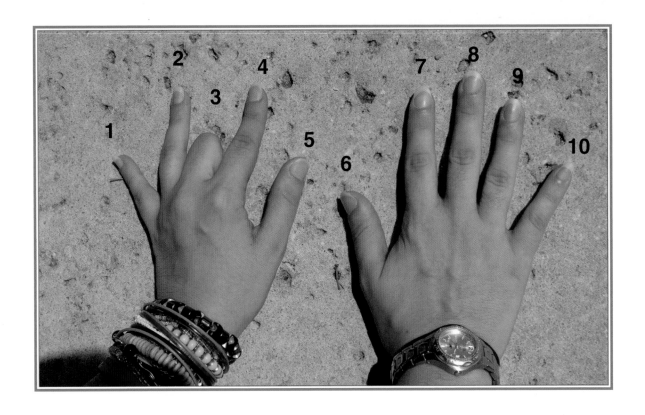

Try the finger trick with nine times three. Curl down finger #3. Do you have two fingers on the left of the curled down finger in the ten's place, and seven fingers on the right?

Three times nine is twenty seven.

3 X 9 = 27

1x9=9	6x9=54
2x9=18	7x9=63
3x9=27	8x9=72
4x9=36	9x9=81
5x9=45	10x9=90

Try the finger trick for nine times four, five, six, seven, eight, and nine. You can check your answers on the nines times table.

Nines Times Table

1x9=9	6x9=54
2x9=18	7x9=63
3x9=27	8x9=72
4x9=36	9x9=81
5x9=45	10x9=90

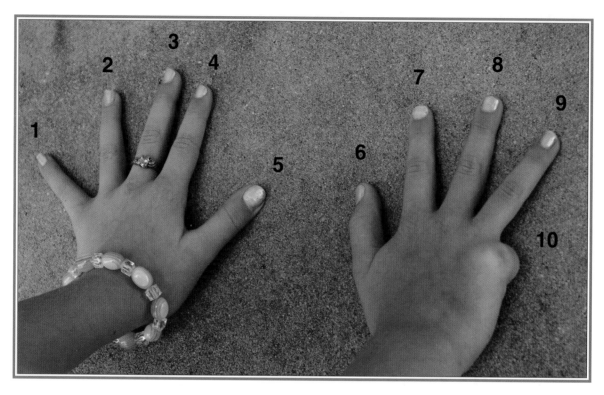

Now you are ready for ten times nine. Curl down finger #10, the pinky of your right hand. How many fingers are on the left of the curled down finger? How many are on the right?

$$1 \times 9 = 9 \qquad 6 \times 9 = 54$$
$$2 \times 9 = 18 \qquad 7 \times 9 = 63$$
$$3 \times 9 = 27 \qquad 8 \times 9 = 72$$
$$4 \times 9 = 36 \qquad 9 \times 9 = 81$$
$$5 \times 9 = 45 \qquad 10 \times 9 = 90$$

If you have nine fingers on the left and none, or **zero**, on the right, you have the answer. Ten times nine is ninety.

$10 \times 9 = 90$

Multiplying Is Like Adding

$$\begin{array}{r} 9 \\ \times\ 2 \\ \hline 18 \end{array}$$
is the
same as
$$\begin{array}{r} 9 \\ +\ 9 \\ \hline 18 \end{array}$$

Remember, multiplying is really adding a number over and over. Two times nine is the same as adding two nines.

When you count by nines, you are adding nine again, again, and again. 9, 18, 27, 36, 45, 54, 63, 72, 81, 90....

Try this problem. 5 X 9 = ?

First, multiply five times nine using the finger trick. Next, check your math by adding five sets of nine. How's your math?

x x x x x x x x x	9
x x x x x x x x x	9
x x x x x x x x x	9
x x x x x x x x x	9
x x x x x x x x x	+ 9
	45

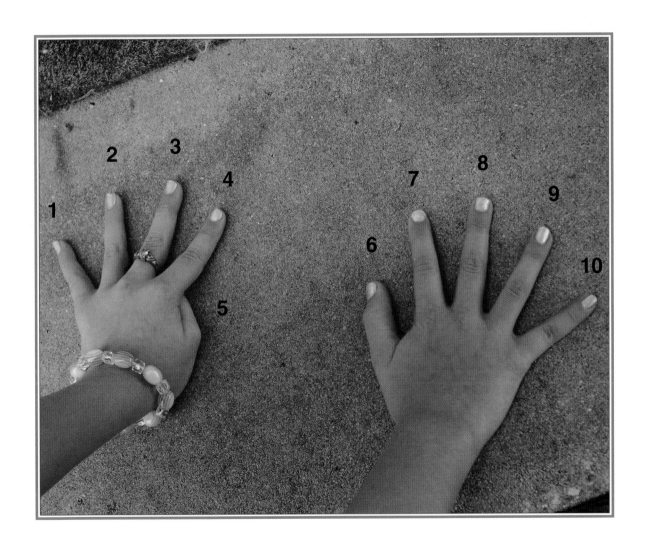

Wouldn't it be great if there were a finger trick for all the other times tables?

Glossary

— the symbol for the word 'number'

handy (HAN dee) — useful

pinky (PINK ee) — a name for the last and smallest finger

represent (rep ree ZENT) — to stand for

zero (ZIHR oh) — none

Index

Further Reading

Dodds, Dayle. *Minnie's Diner: A Multiplying Menu*. Candlewick Press, 2007.

Roy, Jennifer. *Multiplication on the Farm*. Benchmark Books, 2007.

Trumbauer, Lisa. *Double the Animals*. Yellow Umbrella Books, 2006.

Recommended Websites

www.kidsnumber.com
www.resourceroom.net/math
illuminations.nctm.org

About the Author

Marcia S. Freeman loves writing nonfiction for children. Her fifty or more children's books include science, geography, and math titles. A Cornell University graduate, she has taught science and writing to children and their teachers from kindergarten through high school.